W9-BLI-606

Children of the World

My Life in
INDONESIA

Alex Woolf

Cavendish Square

New York

Published in 2015 by Cavendish Square Publishing, LLC
243 5th Avenue, Suite 136, New York, NY 10016

Library of Congress Cataloging-in-Publication Data

Woolf, Alex, 1964- author.
  My life in Indonesia / Alex Woolf.
      pages cm. — (Children of the world)
  Includes bibliographical references and index.
ISBN 978-1-50260-050-9 (hardcover) ISBN 978-1-50260-278-7 (paperback)
ISBN 978-1-50260-051-6 (ebook)
1. Indonesia—Juvenile literature. 2. Children—Indonesia—Juvenile literature. I. Title.

  DS615.W66 2015
  959.8—dc23

2014026347

Editor: Joe Harris
Designer: Ian Winton

All photography courtesy of Denny Pohan / Demotix / Corbis

Printed in the United States of America

Contents

Morning

Hello! My name is Eva. I am ten years old and I live with my mother and father in Soya, a town in Indonesia.

Every morning I get up very early and collect water from the tank for my shower.

We have a water tank next to our house. We use this water for cooking, cleaning, and washing. Water must be boiled to make it safe for drinking.

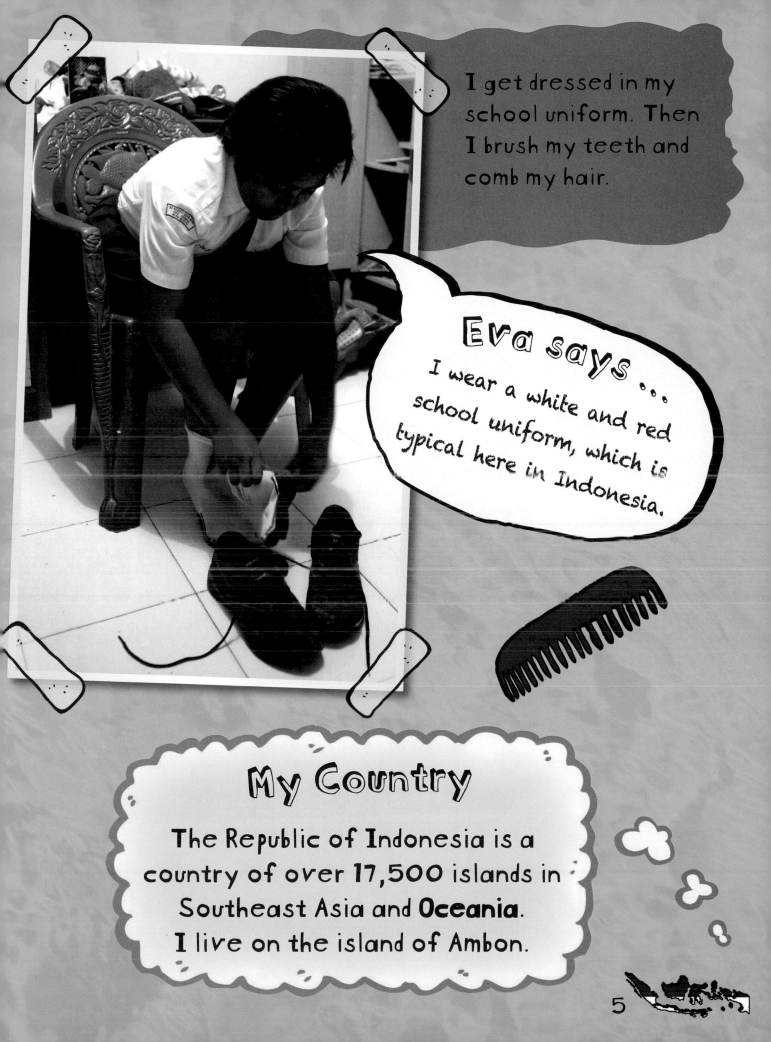

I get dressed in my school uniform. Then I brush my teeth and comb my hair.

Eva says ...

I wear a white and red school uniform, which is typical here in Indonesia.

My Country

The Republic of Indonesia is a country of over 17,500 islands in Southeast Asia and **Oceania**. I live on the island of Ambon.

Breakfast

Mom calls me for breakfast at six o'clock. She ate earlier, because she has to get ready for work. Dad has already left to open the family shop. So I eat on my own.

Mom boils water for our breakfast. She makes us rice with fried tempeh and mie goreng (Me go-Reng).

Tempeh is a traditional food of Indonesia, made from **soybeans**. It tastes delicious fried.

Mie goreng is Chinese noodles. It is made with thin yellow noodles fried with oil, garlic, meat, and vegetables.

Eva says ...

Rice and tempeh are quite enough for me!

Indonesian Food

In my country, we have rice with almost every meal. We might have it with meat or vegetables, and sometimes soup.

Walking to School

At 6:30, I leave for school. By this time Mom has already taken the bus to Ambon City where she works as a **civil servant**.

Eva says...

Mornings are always such a rush!

Soya lies at the foot of the beautiful Sirimau Mountain, which is covered in ancient trees. From the top there are spectacular views of the bay and Ambon City.

When Dad isn't working in the family shop, he does gardening in the neighborhood.

It's a fifteen-minute walk up a steep hill. I usually see my friends and walk with them.

Ambon Island

The island where we live is part of the Maluku Islands in eastern Indonesia. It is green and mountainous. The main city is also called Ambon.

Morning Attendance

My school is called Soya Kota Ambon. In my country, children start school at six years old. I am in the fourth grade.

The bell is rung at seven o'clock for the start of school.

Elementary school is called *Sekolah Dasar*. The school year starts in mid-July and finishes in mid-June. We get two weeks of vacation in December.

10

Eva says ...

We must answer "yes!" in a loud voice when the teacher calls out our names.

After taking attendance, our teacher leads us in morning worship.

School

Next year is my last year at elementary school. After that, I will go to junior secondary school, and I will stay there until I am fourteen.

Lesson Time

Lessons begin at 7:30 and each one lasts about forty minutes. The teachers are quite strict, but we still manage to have some fun during class.

Eva says ...

Here I am with some of my classmates.

I am studying eleven subjects at school. My favorites are natural science, math, and **cultural** arts and skills.

When I started at school, I was allowed to speak my **native language**, Ambonese. But since Grade 3 we get always had to speak in Indonesian.

Time to get to work! These math problems are pretty tough.

Many Languages

Indonesia is a country of over 700 languages. Indonesian (which we call Bahasa Indonesia) is the official language, but most of us speak our native language at home.

10:00 AM

Physical Education

At **10:00**, we have a break from classroom lessons and go to physical education class. Everyone must do PE. It's part of the **curriculum**.

Eva says ...

PE can be tiring, but at least we're outside.

Since I began Grade **4**, we've started to play different sports, such as badminton, tennis, soccer, **futsal**, rounders, similar to baseball, and basketball.

14

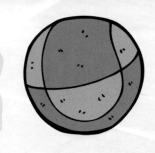

Sepak Takraw (se-PAK ta-KRAW) is another popular sport here. It's like volleyball, but players use their feet, knees, chest, and head to touch the ball, not their hands.

We are practicing *Pencak Silat*, a traditional dance and martial art of Indonesia.

Sport

Indonesians love badminton. We have won many Olympic gold medals in this sport. Soccer, which we call football, is also very popular.

Playtime and Lunch

After some more classroom lessons, we take a break at noon. We go out into the playground for half an hour. At 12:30, the bell rings for lunch.

Eva says ...

My best friend at school is Meiliani.

It is sunny outside. Because we are near the equator, we have a tropical **climate**. It is warm all year. The rainy season lasts from November to March.

I enjoy jumping rope, but I'm not that good at it!

For lunch, we are served nasi uduk (NAH-see oo-doo) (rice cooked in coconut milk) and salad.

Petak Benteng

In this Indonesian playground game, there are two teams and each must defend their 'fort' (it could be anything, like a bench or a tree). At the same time players try to capture the other team's fort.

Traditional Dancing

At two o'clock, we move aside the desks and chairs to create some space so we can practice traditional Indonesian dancing.

Eva says ...
The dances are complicated. It's not easy to remember all the steps.

My country is made up of many different **ethnic groups** and they all have their dances. In fact there are more than 3,000 traditional dances in Indonesia.

Here we are practicing a traditional court dance.

This is the *maluku* (Ma-LOO-koo). Dancing around bamboo poles is fun, but you have to be careful not to trip up!

Indonesian Dance

Our culture has many kinds of dance, from ancient tribal dances to religious and folk dances. The costumes can be spectacular!

Home Time

School ends at three o'clock. I go home, change out of my uniform, and take my bike for a ride.

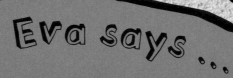

Eva says ...

I love riding around the streets of my town—except for the uphill parts!

I go to school six days a week, and this is always my favorite time of day. I like to play games with my friends.

Sometimes we play a skipping game called *lompat tali (LOM-pot TAH-lee)*, in which we take turns jumping over an elastic rope. Or we might play *bekel*, a game similar to jacks.

Today we're playing *kereleng* (marbles). I'm trying to knock the marble out of the circle.

Kite Flying

On windy days, we go *layang-layang (LIE-yan LIE-yan)* – kite flying. We make our kites from bamboo, waxed paper, and string.

Music Practice

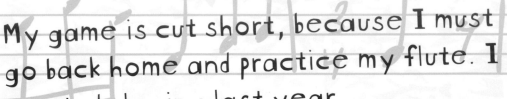

My game is cut short, because I must go back home and practice my flute. I started playing last year and my teacher says I must practice every day.

Eva says ...
I play an Indian eight-hole bamboo flute.

We make all kinds of music in Indonesia, from tribal chants to pop and rock. One of my favorites is a kind of dance music called Dangdut (DANG-doot).

Most Indonesians are Muslim, but my family is Christian. Every Sunday, I sing in the church choir. This evening there is choir practice, so I must hurry to church.

We are practicing some hymns. I love it when we sing harmonies.

Gamelan

Our most famous music is probably gamelan (GAH-me-lahn), which uses drums, gongs, **metallophones**, bamboo flutes, and sometimes singers.

Family Shop

At 5:30, I head over to the family shop to close it up for the evening. It is in the high street, not far from our house.

Eva says ...

I check how much stock we have of the most popular products, then list the ones we're running out of.

Our shop sells sweets, snacks, and soft drinks. It gets very busy around midafternoon when children are coming out of school.

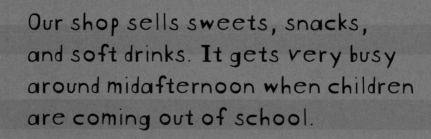

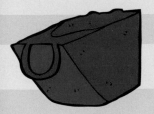

The high street is always a lively place, with **street vendors** selling hot snacks and *becaks (BEH-ka)* (bicycle rickshaws) taking people from place to place.

I lock the door carefully and close the shutters to stop anyone from breaking in.

Indonesian Money

We call our currency the *rupiah*. Sometimes we call it *perak* (silver), as a nickname. There are about **11,000 rupia to a U.S. dollar.**

At Home

When **I** get back home from the shop, **I** do my homework. Tonight, **I** must practice writing English sentences.

Eva says ...

Writing in English is very hard!

When **I** grow up **I** would like to be a doctor. Many Indonesians suffer from diseases such as **HIV/AIDS**, **dengue fever**, and **malaria**. **I** would like to help them.

My aunt works as a nurse in the hospital in Ambon City. She says that unsafe drinking water is a major cause of death in young children. We always boil ours.

My aunt reads me a story on her electronic reader.

My Plans

When I'm fourteen I want to go to a senior secondary school specializing in science and medicine. After that, I hope to go to medical school. The nearest one to Ambon is in Makassar.

Evening Meal

At seven thirty, we sit down to eat a meal of rice, noodles, and dried fish. We talk about what we did today.

Eva says ...

My aunt and cousin join us for the meal.

Mom fried the dried fish with peanuts. This dish is called *teri kacang* (*TER-ee KA-chang*), and it is originally from **Java**.

I'm very hungry after having such an active day!

After we finish eating, I help Mom wash the dishes, then I get ready to go to bed. It's about eight o'clock by now and I'm very sleepy. Goodnight!

Tumpeng

When we celebrate a family birthday, we have a *slametan (SLAH-ment-an)*, or feast. And we cook *tumpeng (TOOM-pung)*, which is a cone-shaped mound of rice surrounded by other dishes.

Glossary

civil servant Someone who works for the government, helping to deliver public services.

climate The weather conditions found in a particular place over a long period of time.

cultural Relating to the arts and achievements of a particular people or nation.

curriculum The subjects that must be studied.

dengue fever A disease of the tropics, caught from mosquitoes. It causes sudden fever and acute pain in the joints.

ethnic groups A group with its own national or cultural traditions.

futsal A form of soccer played with five players per side on a smaller, usually indoor, field.

HIV/AIDS HIV (human immunodeficiency virus) is a virus that can lead to the disease AIDS (acquired immunodeficiency syndrome), which lowers the body's resistance to infection.

Java An island in Indonesia, Java is the world's most populous island with a population of 143 million (2014). The country's capital, Jakarta, is on Java.

malaria A disease of the tropics, transmitted by mosquitoes. It invades the red blood cells. It causes fever, headache, and, in severe cases, death.

metallophones A musical instrument in which the sound is produced by striking metal bars of varying pitches.

native language The language a person has grown up speaking from early childhood.

Oceania An area that covers the islands of the Pacific Ocean and neighboring seas.

soybeans Plants native to Asia, which are grown for their beans.

street vendors People who sell things in the street, either from a stall or van or with their goods laid out on the pavement.

Further Information

Websites

www.ducksters.com/geography/country.php?country=Indonesia
  A single-page profile of Indonesia, full of useful facts.

kids.embassyofindonesia.org/aboutIndonesiacover.htm
  A general introduction to Indonesia, produced by the Indonesian
  Embassy in the United States, with information about the country's
  people, history, geography, language and wildlife.

kidworldcitizen.org/2013/06/23/kids-learn-about-indonesia
  An interesting blog about Indonesia.

www.infoplease.com/country/indonesia.html?pageno=1
  Information about Indonesia's history.

www.timeforkids.com/destination/indonesia
  Facts about Indonesia, including a sightseeing guide, Indonesian
  phrases, and a day in the life of a typical Indonesian child.

Further Reading

Hibbs, Linda. *All About Indonesia: Stories, Songs, and Crafts for Kids.*
  North Clarendon, VT: Tuttle, 2014.

Kalman, Bobbie. *Spotlight on Indonesia.* Spotlight on My Country.
  New York, NY: Crabtree Publishing, 2010.

Roberts, Russell. *We Visit Indonesia.* Your Land and My Land: Asia.
  Hockessin, DE: Mitchell Lane, 2014.

Rush, Elizabeth, and Eddie Hara. *I Is for Indonesia.* Alphabetic World.
  San Francisco, CA: ThingsAsian Press, 2014.

Ryan, Patrick. *Welcome to Indonesia.* Welcome to the World.
  North Mankato, MN: The Child's World, 2007.

Index